ACCORDING TO THE SMALL HOURS

BY THE SAME AUTHOR

POETRY

Windfalls
Minding Ruth

FICTION

Adventures in a Bathyscope
Muesli at Midnight
Lipstick on the Host

PLAYS

The Diamond Body
The Antigone
Exit/Entrance
The House of Bernarda Alba (translation)

AS EDITOR

Immediate Man: Cuimhní ar Chearbhall Ó Dálaigh

ACCORDING TO THE SMALL HOURS

Aidan Mathews

CAPE POETRY

Published by Jonathan Cape 1998

2 4 6 8 10 9 7 5 3 1

First published in Great Britain in 1998 by Jonathan Cape
Random House, 20 Vauxhall Bridge Road, London SW1V 2SA

Random House Australia (Pty) Limited
20 Alfred Street, Milsons Point, Sydney,
New South Wales 2061, Australia

Random House New Zealand Limited
18 Poland Road, Glenfield,
Auckland 10, New Zealand

Random House South Africa (Pty) Limited
Endulini, 5A Jubilee Road, Parktown 2193, South Africa

Random House UK Limited Reg. No. 954009

A CIP catalogue record for this book
is available from the British Library

ISBN 0-224-05125-3

Papers used by Random House UK Limited are natural,
recyclable products made from wood grown in sustainable forests.
The manufacturing processes conform to the environmental
regulations of the country of origin.

Typeset by Palimpsest Book Production Limited
Polmont, Stirlingshire

Printed and bound in Great Britain by
Creative Print and Design (Wales), Ebbw Vale

For Laura

Omnis ab hac cura cura levata mea est
Fall to the work, its careful, careless righting
Ovid, *Tristia*

CONTENTS

VIGIL

ACKNOWLEDGEMENTS

Acknowledgements are due to the editors of the following periodicals:

The Inherited Boundaries (Dolmen), *Irish Times*, *Penguin Book of Contemporary Irish Poetry* (Penguin), *Poetry*, *Poetry Ireland Review*, *Princeton University Library Chronicle*

The author thanks the Arts Council of Ireland for the 1996 Literature Award.

Preface

One branch of apple-blossom has blanked it all out,
The plaque at the granite door that commanded: it is
Forbidden to throw confetti in the grounds of the church;
And the holy-water font has filled wholly with rain now,

Sooty freshwater from some ruined eye-shadow,
Where the boy with Down's syndrome bows on tiptoe
At these vanilla weddings in the invalid car-park
To slide his tongue deeper into his own mouth.

COMPLINE

Do you work wonders for the dead?
Do the shades rise up to praise you?

Psalm 88

HOW WORDS MEET TO MAKE A POEM

There is a green ruin where they gather in twos and threes
Like Pentecostalists in the Soviet Union.
Because they are perfect strangers, they can trust each other,
Speechless at last in the kind sub-zero. A handful,
With one frostbitten foot in front of the other,
Measure the parade-ground like a tightrope artist would
In the small steps that bring us to our knees.

The night before the work is to start for good,
They grow silent. They go silently. Fires are let die
And they breathe in undertones. Stars may or may not,
But the small hours gloss their sleeping bags
Like site machinery under moonlight, straw on the iron,
And where they lie the frost cannot find them out,
The vegetables their bodies bodyguard.

THE ACOUSTIC OF WATER

for a grandmother

In an *Oxford Dictionary of Famous Last Words*
I would pencil in the phrase, 'My waters are breaking',
From one whose mummified hands shook like a water-diviner.

On the hospital wall a font full of holy water
Had dried in the heat of a semi-private death.
Sealed mineral drinks were heaped at a bed with bars.

The sheets were soaking. All that was left to us
Of the Greek New Testament was that change of linen,
The dry white windings and the whiteness of feet.

So too in the nave of the church, flowers from Israel
Stood in a dry oasis, a beached Moses basket,
While we prayed in a heatwave for blessings to rain down.

May you also discover the few proverbial palm-trees,
A well where the saddlebag spurts as you haul it
Up on the windlass-rope like a soggy child in a caul,

And the storyteller at sea in his boat on the lake of Galilee –
Beyond where we are left standing, beyond this landfill
Planted already for ease with shrubs from a desert –

So that his speech can be heard by women with waterjars,
By the shore-dwellers who listen for shoals
And who shelter under an awning of dried-out drift-nets

To fathom the words that move them over the water
Like mist in the evaporations of summer,
Something their mothers had told them their mothers had said.

See how the working women are all ears as they stoop,
How the firewood twitches in their fingers, how they cry out
As the drowning child turns in the womb and dives straight down.

TWO JOHANNINE HYMNS

I EYE-DROPS

Dropping them into my brother's eye
Was like a bomb-bay opening over Germany.
When I squeezed the rubber nipple, ointment dripped
Pear-shapes from a pipette

Like sobs in a cartoon, Egyptian pupils
Raining down on boulevards and department stores
And all the sights of the lit-up city
That you would miss if you so much as blinked.

His cornea was an archer's target
For Robin of Sherwood to start quivering,
A dart-board for the orbiting
Shots of morphine before shut-eye. Lights-out.

When he batted the world in a slow exposure
It took in the whole, telescoped
Ceiling-rose where he had hung Hurricanes
And Lancaster bombers by their ball-turrets,

The light-bulb bobbing in carbon copies
And my double, his three-legged, two-faced brother.
We have filled in long since for the sake of the children
The pond that froze over in a film of oil.

In the language of Greece, of grey-eyed Athene,
I have seen and *I know* are a perfect likeness.
It grows on the pupil. God in a toga
Regarded him daily from a nail on the wall,

From a cyclops Sacred Heart, as he stockpiled
Spectacles like a minor pogrom.
He wore them for those black-and-white newscasts
Of the night-bombing of North Vietnam

When the long rope-ladders descended and ascended
Like the chiselled calendars in a cell
On the open-eyed children of the blind asylum
And were followed at curfew on Christmas Eve

By parachutes full of dolls with eyelids
That cried chemical tears if you tilted them
Upside-down like a full-term baby
Intent on his tunnel-vision, his solo flight-plan.

Twenty years on, an optician
Drops deadweights like pennies on my framed face
Until I can see the writing on the wall
That my brother chalked up with such a dry eye.

Time and tide, they say. *Ebb and flow*, they tell us.
You're stranded in a photographic memory:
Twenty, twenty-one, the length and breadth of a life-guard
Who will only fit in the viewfind if I step back more.

A full foot. Picture it. The automatic exposure,
Those Kodak moments, white breaker after breaker,
And the one eye closing and closing and closing in
Because of the blown sand, an iota of grit.

When my own child buried me there up to my medal
I blinked like the quadriplegic who asked for jelly
And thought of your footsoles quietening in a trolley-cot,
Of the boy who groomed your burial mound with the sea:

With ivy of shore-weed, washed-up, washed-out wreaths,
With coral that the Gulf Stream goes on offering,
Shells in the letters of John and a gull's Holy Ghost feather
As light as the tufts the steel-comb's brush-strokes sifted.

Shutterspeed snapshots. Sand slides from your foot.
Hopper-flies sprint in the stencil of a sock.
From the sand-pile that I pounded on a blond abdomen,
The guard-rail of the bunk above me, a film of dust,

From the blackened insole of a lost winklepicker
And a coffin where the heels crisscrossed like a foetus,
You rest your whole weight upon flesh and blood.
I shoot from the shallows in plastic disposable sandals.

SURGEON AT SEVENTY-FIVE

He has fed a whole family by cutting off breasts.
In under my bed still, like a boy's amazing magazines,
A tool-chest flashes scalpels. Pliers. The suture threads
Of a life-time of lymph glands, of brown, banished planets.
His children's milk-money, life-jackets, globe-trotting tandems,
Began and ended in this monosyllabic culling.

His son opened a book as beeswaxed as Bibles once
At the black-and-white sub-tropical plates of tumours,
Spotlit melanomas on goose-pimpled ghost-bikini tops.
The women's faces were blotted like bar-codes, their teeth bared.
They had taken off their earrings, even. You could see the holes ooze,
And a phone-number inked on a veiny, papercut hand.

In the pin-up year of Stalingrad when the German conscripts
Waded like deciduous woods through the snows of Russia,
Mother Teresa of Avila, the senior theatre sister,
Felt a sword pierce her breast as he parted another one.
I could see the heart, she said. *I could see it beating.*
I wanted to stroke the membrane like the embryo of a baby.

And myself, born with the cross-over milk of my mother
Dribbling upside-down from my useless nipples
On a night when the Milky Way had whitened the Rotunda,
Was weaned on Rider Haggard, on the Holocaust,
On the beautiful bare breast of the priestess Princess
And the doubled-up granny drenching the ramp with her hand on
her heart.

Check them for lumps and they'll love you like mammals,
My glorious gigolo roommate would tell me. *You're home*
When they drop the private pet-names for both their boobs.
Static of cardigans. The thousand nuclear breast-pocket
Ballpoints aimed at the curving globe in our galaxy
Were the mythical here-be-monsters of Krishna's milkmaids

The day I warmed my blue hands on a hot-water bottle
While a girl took off her bra like it was Duccio's studio.
How had my father touched my mother's body
In a room where Jesus pointed to his white-hot chemotherapy?
I woke from my own sleep like an anaesthetic
With a pain in my chest I did not know from Adam.

It is too late now to lie in anyone's breast.
What you hear is the terrible sound that comes from the heart
As my daughter's breasts grow up in a circling world.
They will round on her. My mother's point to the ground,
And my father sags among helium birthday balloons
That bob and brown and wizen and drag at his boots.

DRAWN IN THE SAND

My father at eighty, his birthday an Archduke's black-out,
Roots among headstones now in search of his mamma and dad.
City vixen have rubbed their behinds grandiosely
On the vital statistics of the hunchback of Donnybrook

Who could not rest easy with seventy stacked pillows
Or a wedding shot that showed him the world's weight on his shoulders;
In my grandmother's lap, with its tinfoil of Easter eggs
And the sable tails of stoles, silt decants into antlers.

Their slabstone whitens to a washing-line with the shit of birds
Who have winged it from a monastery in the Atlas mountains;
The cot-death in a shoe-box might double as a bolster,
Stowed like a book of Thomas Cook cheques in the dormitory

Where I imagine her fountain-pen postcard from the Dead Sea
To a sister whose might-have-been beau filled a French sandbag.
'When you step out of the water, you must immediately
Wash yourself clean. Baptisms upstream. The Jordan stops here.'

Spittle-spiders, spared irises, stripped styrofoam cups:
Cider-freaks like glassblowers float condoms among obelisks
Where the living images of my few children presided once
On the first flush-toilet in Irishtown. Sandymount next stop.

My father rises and falls among the tablets of granite
Like a mullah, like the white sea-horses where he scribbled
  with stumps.
Those who were great and great-great – the little, belated knighthoods –
Storm and subside in nursery-plots of scratched Latin dog-tags.

There he is now. He slips among the shadows of evergreens
In a soundless, slow-motion manner. It is always
A tickertape of black and white in the grasshopper newsreels,
The bare-headed dead waving their caps at the tracer-fire,

While his grandchildren are playing in the sandpit I have built them,
Tunnelling passage-graves out of four sackloads of strand,
Patting the mounds like a pregnancy, like a Buddha's belly,
Or building up a breast with a bright bottle-top nipple

Until it's a bailiwick with walls and a freshwater well.
Room for ammunition. Plans for manslaughter. By the time
The old man, lost in the alphabetical cemetery,
Is back where he had found himself before the siren sounded,

It will be in ruins. He follows the writing all over,
The arrowheads of birds on their way back to the desert.
Now his walking stick rattles the iron bars of the clockwise
Turnstile. Now his descendants straighten up in the pit,

Bringing the sand into the house on their hands, their feet,
Leaving it in the sink, on the stairs, on the warm landing,
At the bottom of the bed, in the piled-up pillows even,
The crevices in our faces where we listen and kiss.

LAVA

He has turned the volume down for the other dying men.
Now it is time for the two of them, father and son,
And the dumbfounded volcano spewing from the satellite picture.

If it weren't in colour, it would be a leaf out of Dante,
The same Divine Comedian they had always intended to read
Out loud in the little sabbaticals of the human tragedy.

Now the liquid bullion slides like the brandy flame on a pudding,
The slow syrup of gorse-fires, an electrified landscape:
The boulevards of Las Vegas seen from a lunar crater.

They sit and watch it happen to them in the next continent,
The wooden verandas slipping in stages down the terraces
Like a tray tobogganning off a hospice bed-cover;

And the father phones his ancestors on the TV remote control
While the rescue party prays to a *deus ex machina*
For the combat-veteran pilot of an American helicopter

To evacuate them out of this hell, out of this purgatory,
This unspeakable parody. From the sight of all such
Last things, Lord, restore us to the set of our televisions!

Let the crater cool to an inverted nipple,
And the shrubs elbow their pilgrim way back to the summit
With the parasites that they host for the birds which belong there.

Let the hole fill with what we have added to the water-table,
The children draw a deep breath and sink out of sight
To their face-masks lying face-up on the bed of our tears.

But for now, in the here and now, it is time's eternity,
The fathers spreadeagled or foetal under a sheet,
Like the honeycomb cavities of Pompeii

That the bright sparks filled with a flood of fresh plaster
In what had been lavabos and old stone lavatories
Till the ward condensed around them and made perfect sense.

FATHERLANDS

I ILIAD

In Meyerhold's posthumous production notes
For the first encounter between the father and the son,
Hamlet ascends into the mist like it was Mount Tabor
To find no God Almighty in chainmail and mutton-chops
But a naked daddy frozen to death between the mortars
With his chest-hair white as a baby's bib, his armpits albino,
His wickerwork ribcage a breastplate of agedness,
And his hands in a basket of knucklebones over his disappeared penis.

They sit together. They touch. The boy covers them both
With his cloak that is made and matted from unprotected species,
The fur of the trapped and the bludgeoned, mammalian solitaries
Whose anthropology is in safe distances –
In the starfish fossils of mountains that inch beyond breathing
Or the roots of old sequoias where they dredge up rooftrees –
And the breath condenses on their lips and nipples.
It is the beloved. It is the father at last. Listen to him.

You must imagine Meyerhold in the labour camp. Limelight
From the watchtowers ghosts the columns of a work-party.
The mercury in their mouths detonates below zero.
Their heads are smoking like cattle in this *aurora borealis*.
If there were a mirror or a polished metal biscuit-box
Or a flat button on a guard's greatcoat or a nail-head, even,
He would see his father's face when he was older
With white smoke pouring from his cry, a head above a cloud.

He's all Greek to me now with the vague, venerable
Beginnings of a beard and a paper tank-top
Marked *Property of the Hospital.* Do I tell him
Odysseus begins in the breathless word for a road
And emigrates from there in sand and sibilance
Which turns those living inland into shy islanders?
Telemachus means the end of all such argument.
His breathing lifts like the green wave of an olive branch.
I hold his hand for the first time in his life
And start the archaic catechism of heroic encounter
Since all farewell must take the forms of greeting.

Who are you, stranger? What city watched you grow?
How did your voyage begin and where has it brought you?
Are you travelling over the ocean in search of your homeland
Or were you already at sea when you sailed through Donnybrook village
In a pair of shoes that you softened by sleeping in them?
Did a woman sweeten your sheets with the saltwater smell
Of a child in tears, the leather of oars, and the breakers' long
Unbroken line where the world comes round full circle?
Why was your father your father and your son your son?
And have you seen a god on your way or been seen by one?
Then I break the bread with him. Then I drink the wine.

BIDDINGS

The bidding prayers I wrote for your requiem Mass
Have given up the ghost in their faint-hearted photocopies
To a woman's subcommittee and a presbytery sideboard.
The surplus lies in staples here among my remaindered fiction –
That paperback remnant, a tongue-tied refugee people! –
With this one black-and-white photograph of a woman in lemon
Who will wait for forty days before she speaks of it:
The thermonuclear thing, the sum of my embryo,
Shaped like a mushroom-cloud between her corset and cartilage,
A supernova's cyst on the screen in Radiography.
It will become a middle-aged head on middle-aged shoulder-bones.

I store it *in camera* between the peace-prayer of Saint Francis,
Charge-cards like missal-markers and an organ-donor I.D.
So that some complete stranger in the cardiac ambulance-crew
May take heart from it one night as the wailing villages bypass,
And intercede for the dying: the photographer's shadow, her husband;
The shadow behind her, the house that has taken her breath away;
While the shadow she pitches, its elongated abdomen –
It is sunrise again on the Feast of the Crushed Invertebrate
When even the millipede cannot be trodden upon
And the microbe blooms in the blue planet of a tear-drop –
Petrifies the border like the carbon of a kimono.

EX CATHEDRA

The woman for whom Jesus can do nothing at all
Is strapped into a wheelchair by her ankles and wrists
With her anus angled above the commode *ex cathedra*.
A ponytailed prodigal hugs her drip-stand at Christmas.

Patted, the skin of her forearm blackens and bleeds.
The hair has slipped from her scalp in a plague of Egypt
Until she becomes a pharoah who was once a Hebrew slave-girl,
A mystery of kisses decanted into a mummified skull.

Balance began it. Then hearing and speaking and sight.
It is too hard now to swallow Holy Communion or water.
She remembers instead the sound of each door in her childhood:
She thinks that the telephone-book is the altar-list of the dead.

Her own dead children are playing cards in a labour ward;
Their hair has grown out at last over neat nautical stitches.
From time to time they look up and talk into the camera.
She has always wanted a mute to interpret the holes in their faces.

As the last and least of her sons minds his own business
The children with terminal cancer stagger through Disneyland,
The candles slot in the cardboard hand-guards of Lourdes,
And the city runs its marathon miles from the place

Where the prestige sicknesses point with their starting pistol.
He has walked away from the television in tears
At the blind boys singing their hearts out in Jerusalem
Or the woman who takes in hot food through her letterbox

But this is between the two of them, placenta and afterbirth -
The overhead lighting that lays him out like a waterless tract,
And the fuselage of her blue-blooded whirlwind
Men watched in their rear-view mirrors like Moses watched God.

EYE WITNESS

The first month of his mother's coma entranced him.
He sat on her bed and he told her his life-story,

Everything seen and unseen. The works. And he wept.
He had never heard the like of it for loveliness.

The second month he speed-read a novel to almost half-way.
It falls open today at the scene of sexual intercourse.

Lastly he browsed in the home-and-holiday pages;
His arms ached like Christ on the Cross from the spread newspaper.

Which was why, in the broadsheet blur, he did not see it:
The exodus from her eye like a sleigh in the desert,

Or the slim, minimal shining of the line that it left there
As if this were enough, to travel a time in gravity –

Canaan, Israel, Palestine, all holy lands
Where lovers go in and out of each other like kitchens,

Their mouthfuls of God, their beeswax bodies on fire! –
While the student nurses agree with their upside-down watches.

The books insist they were physiological waste.
The doctors dilate on the autonomic phenomena

Of the lachrymal duct. Anything else is eye-wash –
Like the pump-action blubberings of the Virgin's statue,

Her crocodile tears in the hoodwinked basilica
Where he had stared so intently at her hand-tinted pupils

He did not see through the stream of pilgrims around him:
Glaucoma, cataracts, contact lenses dissolving,

A glass too full to drink from without spilling,
Water turning to tears in the witness of sightseers.

ALL BURIALS ARE AT SEA

Boats have been lifted down into the water all week now:
The centre-boards, the cabin cruisers, the great ocean-going,
And the toddlers are making heirlooms with their hands in the breakers.
Theirs is the drift of where he stands, my old shore-dwelling father
At his sea-front dormer window with the Second-World-War binoculars
Waiting for his life to well up like a submarine
So he can row out towards her, towards the dots and dashes,
Through the rowlocks' chronic bronchitis to the air of sirens,
And be among his countrymen at the bottom of the sea,
Feeling the pain of the oars like the start of a stroke in his shoulder
And sad for the living, for those left behind in the photographs.

He has stowed you in a little hardwood boat, a dug-out almost,
With a prayer-book full of your war kids shrieking Cheese
And a picture of Jesus dead to the world on a fishing-net, foetal,
While the wino mariners wail and the waves turn over the pages.
But the one that I cannot fathom floated in wetness before me,
A girl on a strand who is copying swimsuit stars in a movie,
The sweethearts of soldiers and sailors, a diver with jewellery on.
She has been buried two miles inland and two metres down
Where the tiny crustacean dust rises and rinses the wormholes.
For nothing omits it, that moment of coral, the violet, visible light
Or the jellyfish belling with joy through the dormitory suburbs.

CARYATIDS

for my mother

I

Lie down beside me
As you had to once in a West of Ireland cottage
The night the fetch from Newfoundland flipped the storm-window
And the sea went mad at the sight of itself. Spray fled from it howling
Like a naked file of reprisals being bullhorned into a quarry –
The stencils of sock-elastic, the pinch-marks of tortoiseshell glasses!
Water-rats wolfed a punnet of poison above my worst asthma.
Wind in the rafters whined for a steroid. Behind my medicines –
Tablets, capsules, ampules; the drooled, useless nebulizers –
I could scent you beside me all that time in the darkness,
Not the talc and toilet-water, your chapped wrists rooting in basins
Till your hands smelled of ammonia mixed with atomisers,
But something before that, some more ancient enlistment,
Intended, tender, a presence hidden by firelight
With a Mesopotamian shadow that soared to a height behind her
And would not stand for less.

II

Lie down beside me
As we did in a garden later between two flowering territories –
Beyond our apricots the lawn belonged to France the fatherless
Where the war-graves crisscross endlessly in a knitting pattern;
And over the raspberry bushes of a heat-haze in Donnybrook
Soviet tom-tits intercepted all alien greenfly
In the only part of the motherland that was not flesh and blood.
Ambassadors in chains. Our commonwealth of littleness.
We were dressing a washing-line, a pavilion of white flags,
Old-fashioned underwear, blouses, slips and pillow-slips,
The clockwise windings for wounded heads, a breathing-space.
We were talking about our dead and the Resurrection,
As if there were nothing between us except our bodies,
As if we were two distinct persons taking the same singular verb
Like God the Father and Jesus in the weird Greek of Saint Paul's
Shalom and Amen to the mammals.

THE PLOT THICKENS

Three lives of a grave. The first is flowers
With copperplate pet-names on the cellophane igloos
And a mist like the eggs of spiders in a waterproof watchface.
She pots them, plants them – the young widow, the old orphan –
Waiting till the rain has stopped before she stands up soaked
With today's date on her knees where she kneeled on newsprint.

The second is gravel. See-through sackfuls of it
Are sold by a boy who's never heard of hundredweights.
She wears her kitchen gloves to even it like a horsehair blanket
And hides the flowerpots behind bushes at the red-brick back-wall
Among hundreds of other helmets with holes, an army-surplus stack,
Mycenaean cradle-cap from the *National Geographic*.

The third is the grass – no adjectives – with a spittle spider
On its own impossible hypotenuse across a crevasse
And weeds that might have been pills in the language of Asia.
She scrapes the bird-shit from the headstone with a fifty-pence piece
And has nothing to clean the coin but a long receipt
Of the faint and detailed messages in the cool of the boot.

ALL SOULS, ALL SAINTS

All souls, all saints. They will each come home to us –
Denstone and Tess and Gerry, the great good Gus too,
My brother, my sister even, pavilions of the ill.
They will rise up in their graves in the shrouds they were buried in,
The sportscoats and blazers, the bow-ties, the Donegal tweeds,
And sit on the boundary wall of Deansgrange cemetery
With their legs dangling in the bright, new-fangled burglar lights
Like bathers trailing their green calves in a swimming pool.

They will be watching us as we go on watching television,
Star Trek say, for the sake of the argument, the spaceship *Enterprise*
Surging up towards their photographs in Victorian silver
Where the house-plant may be allergic or only hibernating.
They will bless us and save us as we sit there in my book of hours.
In every part of Dublin horse-troughs will fill and flow over,
The streets will shine like Italian canals with the oils of healing
And the warm cart-horses of breadmen and milkmen cross the
washed city
As quietly as reindeer, a migration of solstice trees,
With their hooves in headscarves, in the hoods of anoraks,
Mantillas, skullcaps, trilbies, orange Christmas hats,
Fibreglass wigs for the smiling terminal women.

What are they saying out there in our deaf-and-dumb language -
The language of Shakespeare is the talk of Junior Infants -
As they sit on the boundary wall between keystone and cornerstone?
As they watch your face light up in the light of the fridge
Or a child, with her ankles crossed like a *foetus in utero*,
Like the feet in a crucifixion, make a fist of her first joined writing?
Like Howard Carter, crawling on all fours to the keyhole,
And straining to feast his eyes on the tomb of Tutankhamen,
They are saying: It is wonderful. Wonderful. I can see wonderful things.

THE SENTENCE OF HISTORY

The boy in his Holy Communion whites
With the snake draped from his collarbone like a stole
Is as dead and gone as his tired, retiring granddad
Grounded beside him in the Zoological gardens;
And the adolescent whose penis has gone and straightened
To bring him to his knees in a south-facing veranda
While he dribbles sun-oil like gunpowder on his mother's legs
Is as much amino acids as the children's crusade –
He's left sperm in Constantinople, pus in Istanbul,
Tears from a panic attack in Simon Peter monastery,
Skin from the hand that he writes with on a skillet,
Toe-nails and fingernails in a flat in Palo Alto,
His shit and urine over half the known continents,
Plus blond hair, brown hair, grey hair, white, down the sinks
  of spiders

Where he goes on still washing his hands of everything
But the isobars at the tips of his fingers
That have hardened at this point like any guitarist's
From the air of earth and water, from the sheer sound of it
Magnifying flesh the way a waterblister boosts
The scale of his prints going round and round in circles.

RELICS

The last breath of Saint Joseph in a bottle
And a white tail-feather of the Paraclete –
Gas bric-à-brac that tickled us pink
On our walkabout in the Lateran Basilica.
The ticket-stubs are still stuck in the *Blue Guide*,
Mementoes of the side-kick in your pot-belly.

The sale at Sotheby's later
Of a pair of Jayne Mansfield's opaque stockings
Veiled from our view the sight of ourselves
As we filed past moon-rock in a crystal ball
In the hall of the vast American embassy
Where I will queue again as an alien
When I leave for the States with coral strand in my sneakers
And a stained ivory souvenir of your shoreline.

Meantime, our children's milk-teeth
Have turned the colour of worry-beads in my bureau
And there's no leather-smell on the vulcanised shoe
A toddler wore when she stamped her mark on the world.
At my godmother's executor's sale
A white mantilla is auctioned as a bird-cage cover.

I wash my hands of you when we've made love,
When we receive each other under both threatened species.
Our bodies are not what they were nine months ago, even,
And my eyesight has altered accordingly
To whoever watches the world through my dead brother's corneas
And purifies its waters in his patient kidney.

How then can I stop our two-year old child
Breathing as lightly as a feather on a pane of glass,
And leaving there the shape of a mouth in mist
Or circles from her fingertips on the solid transparency,
Bullet-holes of heat like an exit wound?

CAPITALS

for Lucy at five

The fruit of the tree of the knowledge of good and evil
Hops from the horsehair wig of Isaac Newton
Onto the kitchen table that we have sanded and stained.

You are shaping Annie Apples with your likely left hand.
'Aaahh,' you say, 'Aaahh,' as if a spatula
Were testing for tonsilitis, a hurt in the throat,

While I am feeling my way at the word-processor,
As dumbfounded as the time your mother entered me
With her vegetarian tongue in the den of my mouth.

The words for *shit* and *breadloaf* quicken and die
At the touch of a key. The sentenced lines are snowed under
Like the bridle paths that tunnelled to Mesopotamia;

But 'Aaahh,' you say, 'Aaahh,' in the Alpha and Omega
Of the trees with their collars and ties, the service station,
And the dead day chalked for hopscotch on the tarmacadam.

Who told me I was naked? My father with books,
My wife in so many words I was speechless. I dressed
In the pleats of her flesh, her Fahrenheit, and I took on the world.

A cormorant's feather ends here as a lead pencil,
Your graphite fistful; the blunted, numb nub of it
Pupates from a caterpillar stick to butterfly shavings

As the page fills like a fruit-tree with the apples of your eye:
Amens and Alleluias, that amorous, stammering Aaahh
My mother used as a code-word for defecation.

Listen, pet, to what I am not saying. Listen to the sound
Of the Indo-European sobbing in our windpipes,
To the church-mice in our pencils like a chest infection.

And which of us will list them alphabetically,
Oceans of room in our washing-machine, the skin of our teeth,
And the gravity of windfalls among all footprints,

Obituaries bedded in the grates of fires on day fourteen,
And the yellow beak of the blackbird before the bulletin
Cutting through the darkness like a paper-knife?

SEA-CHANGE

for Laura at ten

I throw a shilling in the deep end for my daughter
And she brings up a Victorian penny from the Land War
I was handed in change on a bus the year of the moon-landing.

The coin spins in an arc at her misted snorkel.
Now it's a Kennedy half-dollar from her great grand-uncle
Who read chunks of the *Summa* at the battle of the Somme.

Another! she cries. Another! And her legs are gone on me
Until I rewind the handstand in the viewfinder
To watch my dead brother stream back to the diving-board

Feet first, high and dry, his straight sleepwalker's arms.
More! she says. Empty everything out of your pockets!
And I cast my small change in, my house-keys,

My wedding ring, the mercury in my mouth,
And she brings it all back to me in the silver of water,
Holding a haul at her chest where her breasts will well up

Someday to the good, the ongoing, the undergone,
Things we have sunk foundations in, shallows and sandbars,
Our finite, teeming, time-consuming Venice.

CAMERAS

The first photograph will always have the last word.
One of Haussmann's avenues for a numbered Napoleon
Faces up to a century of authorised postcards
As the boulevards widen to prevent any barricades.

You would almost expect the late great, dated Chevalier
To dander with a malacca among the callipered saplings
And raise the rooftops like a skylight in a doll's village
Where any lead figure over, say, sixty – for this is 1838 –

Knows the pursuit of happiness depends on concord,
And slips medicinal sherry to the concierge.
But the street's empty. Light draws it in pencil.
The blots here are not horse-dung but the motions of time.

A straight line turns the corner into a no-go zone,
The masonry of the tear-gassed, the baton-charged,
A bald-headed woman among her spitting images,
Smart photographers shooting those about to be shot.

The boy who stood in sandals in the middle of that May
Flicking a postcard back and forth like a hand-mirror
As if he were a prisoner signalling to a rescue party,
Had found his subject mattered. It was a matter of time.

When he bent the postcard backwards, the woman's swimsuit
Parched on her terracotta breasts like amphoras.
Everything stopped. Trains stood still in their tracks.
The sleepers stretched in a dormitory to the horizon.

Around him to left and right the streets had emptied.
The long-haired children had gone in search of the helmeted.
He had lost sight of his parents at the moment of pleasure
And was condemned now to canopies, closed shutters, the cleared

Incoherence of streets where nothing was stirring
Except his body. It ran ahead of him, a standard-bearer,
Through sand-bags, body-bags, a landscape of slogans,
The history of skin and bones, our skeleton key,

To the advent legends of flesh and blood where we build
Our bungled models of children and grandchildren.
He is miles from where he began. He begins again now.
He turns a right angle into the first known photograph

And the whole thing is laid before him in three dimensions.
The shadow of a man having his shoes cleaned,
The shadow of the shoe-shine on his knees before him.
The solid, visible windows framing a view of beds

In darkened rooms where things come slowly to light
Like the wallpaper pattern welling up under a fresh coat –
The tongues of boots, newspaper strips in chamber-pots,
Children believing daylight out of the shade.

TELLING THE TIME

At the going, going, gone of the television Angelus
His five sons synchronise their Swiss watches;
And at half-past six spoons on a kitchen gong
Beat a Beethoven's Fifth up four carpeted flights

To the rooms where children are dating their homework,
March the whatever, AD '69.
They pencil it in. Their mother signs in ink
The time given to English, and the ink dries as she writes.

Over each desk there is a clock and a crucifix,
An Advent calendar blackened like a bingo card
And a Count of Monte Cristo series of small
Horizontals adding another week on the wallpaper

To a sum I can never arrive at this time round.
God is among us hourly on the half-hour here.
The women, bred in a mass of wafers and hosts,
Fold their mantillas to aprons for oven scones

And the priest props his wristwatch beside the chalice:
His arm has worn its inscription down to *aeterni*.
When I douse the candles after the midday Solemn
Stick-insects chitchat still in its sooty matchbox.

My mother orbits an egg-timer to test hard spellings:
Age, gauge, language. The hourglass chokes
In the steam of the ladled world. The clockface clouds.
Only time can tell us now where the time has gone to.

And my father sits for ages as if for a portrait
With the caterpillar tracks of the strap on his wrist
While Countess Annie Labuntur in the speaking clock
Ticks him off from her blindcraft cockpit in Greenwich.

Now I would set my own watch by the grandfather clock
My grandfather boasted was his bright black coffin
And by the sports stopwatch my dead brother placed
On the starting block of a school-cap salty with sweatstains.

The watchstrap stencil on my suntan ghosts
Two tags I brought home from a lying-in hospital.
Things I have counted on, things that are numbered,
Watchchains and cuckoo-clocks and all such compasses

That quiver between true time and magnetic
And join their hands at midnight as at midday,
Are the silver of angels, coins that are notched like winders
That the blind may treasure the tips of their fingers forever

And the whole time temporary secretaries stir,
The churchbells lift the children off their feet
In peals of laughter to the blue beyond; and the swimmers
Wade into the water in their wet, waterproof bodies.

ENTRIES

Each evening for a summer he wrote in his diary:
Went to the wood. And every morning after
Two conifers and a crab-apple were his interior,
Chapel and lab and sleeping bag and launch pad.
Kennedy came to him there on his hands and knees,
James Bond and Francis Xavier and Che Guevara.
He had saved all the women and children in the world
And would be shot at cock-crow in Kilmainham
After being breastfed by his torturer, Françoise Hardy.
When he looked up, Victorian appleblossom
Loomed like the canopy of underwear in the kitchen.
He lay along the division of grass and moss,
One half of him in the ticklish tobacco of laps
And the other in the cool coma of evergreens.

Up there behind the glasshouse, above and beyond him,
His parents sat and said nothing in the cemetery of wood
Among the arms of couches and the legs of chairs
And the stairwell of old banisters where the boards sagged
Like the eggbox softness of sand over an atrocity.
But he walked the tramline stones in his sandalled feet
To a brick wall, to a hose that danced like cobras
When he opened the tap, to an anti-clockwise world,
The saddle smoothness of the fork in the apple tree.
Went to the wood. And in that wooden horse,
He entered Troy, Rome, the headquarters of Spectre
And Felicity O'Leary from Number Seventy,
While his parents discussed what the newspapers told them to
With clothes called *Missed her* and *Miss Us*, their imaginary friends.

GUARDIANS

Vowels in the flue of the chimney meant that the Nile
Had floated a basket of chicks into our breastwork,
And the cock crowing at the corner of Ailesbury Road
Made my mother weep like Peter when his tears baptised him.

So of course I could imagine an angel with wings
That folded up like my father's maps or the wings
Of the priest at prayer who was climbing Jacob's ladder
While I tied his soutane in the slip-knots of a sheet anchor.

For three years I slept on the edge of the bed
To leave room for my Greek guardian from Reykjavik.
He was too actual even to be thought about.
When I woke, he had made his side and gone out quietly

With a soundless swoosh of the ironing boards on his back.
Then the Egyptology of chicks would start like static
And the rooster in the lane between the embassies
Produce my mother with the board from Monopoly –

Our own unrivalled road on the home-straight to Go.
What would the wizards of Waddington think of a cock?
And the guardians of the peace, ascending, descending,
Butts lighting their hands like a shrine in the small hours?

My air-hostessing sister had the sky-high lifestyle.
Her underwear clouded my evenings with cumulus nimbus,
The good news of the Kingdom of Heaven,
Like a rope made out of bedsheets let down from Paradise

By an angel with a head for depths and a nose for smells
Below and beneath the odours of sanctity;
And I would slither with him along that umbilicus,
The slips and halters, long, unladdered wisps,

To the bird's nest in our grate one Saturday morning
With human hair in the plaits and quarter-inch tape,
Or the high-stepping cock crossing the road with his harem
While a priest flicked holy water on the new Triumph Herald.

Somewhere in all of this I would ground my stand
On a wing and a prayer, on the back-carriage of messages
Brought to a tradesman's entrance, a high-flown pantry
Porthole: soda-bread and pine-wood toilet freshener,

Today's news in tomorrow's fire, a phoenix singing,
The family I have buried like so many parachutes,
Angels, the gospel truth; and me waking at cock-crow
To the company of one barely breathing, to a clean sheet.

VIGIL

More than those who watch for the morning;
more than those who watch for the morning.

Psalm 130

PATIENTS IN THE WAITING ROOM

Caption the legend. Swear they are
Models in a life-class at an art school somewhere
With that tiny ticking of heaters, the seething
Pilot of a gas-plaque like the wind under a weatherboard

And the three of them sitting so quietly there
That a bluebottle might ship its wings on a signet ring
Or the moisture at the edge of a nostril waver but not wobble.
The students spread out around them in a half-moon, and begin.

Chalk and charcoal. Under that camel-hair coat,
Her breasts have elastic pinch-marks, lines from a draughtsman's notes.
The isobar marks on her feet from the moccasin's double-knot
Will still be a figure of eight at the end of every session

As the sighing chair where she sat fills up the slump in the cushion.
The last man in is weeping behind the partition wall
While the other remains with *Time* and *Life* in his lap.
It's late too. Lights occur to the avenue. Rush-hour traffic

Circles and encircles the bumper world. A janitor
Pictures the pretty one who had to be helped to her feet –
Anaesthesia in her buttocks and down the side of her face
As he covered her in the old candlewick dressing-gown –

And locks up now by the light in the light-switch panel.
The portholes wiped in the stopped upstairs of buses
Zero in on that Bedlam as a timid Advent,
A Bethlehem even, blackening like an Old Master

Into oils and oil-lamps. The waiting room draws in
Eyes that the rain has ruined like watercolours,
While the neo-classical husbands and girlfriends and gods
Have nowhere to stop and go on circling the square.

AT THE NURSES' STATION

To property:
One three-quarter-length cavalry overcoat;
Sand-coloured pine-needle corduroy trousers
And a pair of desert-boots soled with odour-eaters.
Veteran leather briefcase (contents: one skipping rope);
Keys on a key-ring with the metal capital A.

To pharmacy:
Tricyclic anti-depressant capsules (forty),
Muscle relaxants, major tranquillizers (*ditto* approx.),
Non-prescription mixed analgesics (*circa* one hundred),
And two additional Ventolin inhalers which may be stored
Pro tem at the nurses' station on the closed male ward.

To laundry:
Shirt (worn at collar and cuffs on admission); all underwear –
Argyll socks, medium Y-fronts, one St Michael's vest –
And a lady's handkerchief that may/may not be heirloom,
Therefore advise possible dryclean? Please provide
Interim toiletries. He is convinced that he smells.

Miscelaneous (Cellaneous? Anneous? Miss?):
Wristwatch, wedding-ring and miraculous medal Mary,
Hair from a sweetheart and/or saint in cellophane,
Nicotine pastilles, a multiple-organ donor-card,
Polaroid of a child touching an elephant's trunk,
Plus a pocket-diary that stinks of roll-on deodorant.

Its pages for the next sixteen months are already
Black and blue with commitments that cannot be broken.

IN A WARD NAMED FOR SAINT PAUL

A boy born to my mother on the day of my birth
Would be thirty now with an orchard of daughters
And a Mayfest when the oldest had her period.

The storm has made the alarm tell more than it knows.
The wind drags the chestnut trees for our children
And pastes debris from the bonfires back on the branches.

An olive tree planted on the day of my birth
Would be ready at last for the hands of its hairdressers.
Was the Son of Man the Son of God? Child's play.

Was the Son of God then God the Son? Men's talk.
The stone that Sisyphus rolls like a dung-beetle
Is not the stone of the tomb but a stone's throw away

Where someone has been petrified by the kiss of life
Like a child lifted up to a corpse's aftershave
And its fumes of plum pudding where the lip bristles.

The body of Christ pales in comparison to a negro's palm.
My barefoot footsoles blacken. Once I thought
The past of *I write* was *I wrought.* Imagine me that.

The trees die and are dressed as tables, as toilet seats,
In the Anglo-Saxon shorthand for Resurrection.
I went out one time to the funeral games of my jargon

With a child in my addled lap to be christened
In the name of five vowels and one anthropomorphosis.
Now the hard sayings call for silence, silence, silence.

Now I am mum in the college of monologues,
A tortoise in the March hare's slipstream
Like the speed of sound shadowing the speed of light.

THE WATER DRUM

If it were not for God, the beloved,
Water would freeze from the bottom up, from the bed.
He wrote the laws of physics on one side of a sheet
But did not perish the thought of the poor fishes.

It has been months since I failed to rise to you
At the miniature, motorised waterfall. A trout in a pool,
I have stood still for the ornamental tremor
Of a wooden bell in a chapel at bread-breaking.

Those murky images the ultra-sound showed us
Of our child submerged in the grey pond of your belly –
She had gills then and a fin in the small of her back.
Now she's a fish out of water, a floundering asthma face.

Something must have flowed for her to surface.
You could see it under the microscope at the tests,
A glittering, illiterate migration
That went wading out of its depth into the tall shallows.

Maybe it'll all come right like the Mediterranean
Where you left our sandals side by side at the shoreline
Among watercolour nets, and the next day they were dry.
Maybe you'll see me make a great splash yet,

Diving off the springboard of the sanatorium
Like a Nordic champion, like a javelin aimed upstream.
Meantime, my mouth has moon-face ulcers in it
From being landed and landed and thrown back in again –

The nurses rinse my gums with the taste of ebb-tide
On a strand where seaweed popped like frost that time
The Gulf Stream hugged us in its green bedspread
And sardines led us, like the monks once, to the whales' chancel.

Break the ice on the water-barrel, love.
Christ has filled the molecules and fulfilled them
With something other than us. Even the algae are
Green with another Creation, a watered-down world

Like the liquid and steam of our kitchen extension
With those thumb-tacked, wavery, slurred instamatics
Of the colourless sea where the dolphin had dived
In the green freeze-frame of a split-second before.

Someday we three will breast it to the air-hole
And hang there by our mouths like high-wire artists
In the fish-net print of their falls to the safety mesh.
Children will clap till their hands burn with the cold.

Somewhere you test the water with your fingerprints
Till it reaches room temperature for a baby's wash
And I freeze from the bottom up, from the bed in sheets
To the plate-glass shatter-proof window beside myself

Yet holding on, holding my breath to hear them,
The women at the river in the dumbfounded small hours,
Pounding the floodplain white with the palms of their hands,
Humming the world awake for the sake of breakfast.

PENELOPE

The nightmare continues all day until his sleeping pills.
Their hall, stairs and landing are like an apothecary's
With legal tablets and camouflaged chloroform flagons.
Fanged bottle-tops dribble tangerine stalactites.

At night when he bunks in his body's drugged gondola,
She sits in front of her future like a dressing-table
And works at the shape of whatever is looming there.
She is weaving the fibs of their courtship to a work of fiction –

He is home from the wars, the scar where no one can see it,
His expression as peaceful again as when he's sedated.
His shadow fades from his face and hands like a suntan
And the smell of their children impregnates the banisters.

Truly, truly, she tells it. This is hard work, it is heart work.
In the morning, the threads are picked off her blue wrists,
The stitches removed. The scab slides on its gum
Like an eyelid. He wants to be breastfed, force-fed, fed to the fish.

He has learned that a sea-mile is not a land-mile, repeat,
That he must be a Trojan now who handcrafted the gift horse;
And that none of it – shipwreck, atrocity, prayer,
The dead pulling at his genitals from their slippy limbo –

Is more insuperable than the school-run on a school day
And a bath filling with home-made white wine, slowly.
For her Homer has nodded. She has looked up a closed book
Where ravel and unravel mean one and the same thing.

OVEN GLOVES

Hers were a souvenir from Cyprus.
She must count on her stumps now to carbon-date
The burns that have blackened her map of the island.
It's smoke without fire to the bowing woman.

The odd day, baking for the children,
She can smell the oven down by the harbour,
The fumes of bread through the chinks in the blinds
As he rose and fell in the dormitory camp-bed

Who has tossed and turned now to a new pharmacy
From her leavened aphrodisiacs –
The breadloaves blessed and broken in half,
Soaked in the grease of plates, the acids of wine,

And the crusts sown among sick pigeons –
Though once he would not have washed his hands
So lightly of the flour that gloved them
Or the sweat from her pleats on the moons of his nails.

A PRAYER FOR RAIN

Slabstone of the cold hot-water bottle woke me,
Bloated between us like the might-have-been baby
Whose Jewish names I listed in a lock-up ward
Ten years ago. Eli, I said, Eli, at the thought of him
Peeing up in the air like the green spring of a palm tree.
My father rode in a toga through that sobbing cubicle:
His hospital syringes were my water-pistols once.
Shoot! I pour it out in the bidet. Aroma of rubber,
The packhorse hooves of our four feet on a bridle path.
You may be asleep. The wineskin flattens in farts. A banal gallon
That might have dissolved in tears over Galilee drifts
To a kindergarten sandpit somewhere in Odessa, say.
I could increase and multiply all of this
But the Jordan has emptied forever into a wash-hand basin.

In the hospital someone has stained his moccasins
And dries them in the warm hand-dryer with his trousers down.
His criminal penis moistens like a sty. I can see him, weeping.
A boy walks into the rain with his watering can.
Mothers are grooming their babies with their tongues
Or their hands are deep as surgeons in the kitchen sink,
And the washing lines are bedouin in the drizzle.
Our bedclothes pitch their tent among the settled people.
Freckle the face of the earth, my illness, Eli!
Fractions of wet, of sperm and perspiration,
Bleach to the taste of salt on the bridge of my glasses.
In the breath between the windshield and the windshield wiper
Let fall the shapes of grieving as refreshment; rain
At the snail's pace of our most colourless lives.

THE CEILING ROSE

I paint a picture of it all over my ceiling last thing at night
From the first impressions of life to the Last Judgement –
The apocalypse of flesh, the deepest unveiling:
The buttocks opening out into a vast vellum manuscript
And the soft, strong, elongated penis like a bread-roll.
I fly by the seat of my pants in an alfresco *agape*.
There's God the Father reaching out to Adam
Like the old aviator and the boy astronaut meeting in Cincinnati
When Orville Wright autographed a napkin for Neil Armstrong.

Comes the morning. Between cock-crow and sunrise,
I can smell my body before I inhale it. Underneath me
My scaffolding's in ruins. Paint on the floor strews pigeon-shit
And the dead, dumbfounded popes like the crowd at Canaveral
Are watching a bolt from the blue, a fireball in free-fall.
And here's our apparatchik, the Trouser-maker, shinnying up
To tog those naked people out as painted women,
To force the prophets into the boxer shorts and buttondown shirts
He found in the fiasco of my chest of drawers.

TRIPTYCH FROM A CLINIC

I ONE IS AFRAID OF THE DARK ALL DAY LONG

'The tiny report of pottery was what I hoped for,
Papyrus wrapped up in itself like a fortune-cookie's horoscope
And the scrolled white breadloaf of a fresh fifth gospel.
My dad in that pothole in Europe with the prehistoric paintings
Prayed in his head a whole Mystery for the poor pre-humans
As if he was reading the Mass in the Church of the Holy Sepulchre;
But the echo returned his password as a slow hand-clapping.
When I was his age, I was older. I wormed on my hands and knees
Ahead of all my descendants into the wet cavity
Of the toilet-smell of a cave at low tide, telling them
My tunnel-vision of Orpheus, Sesame, holes that are grottoes.
Then I rose up out of it in the landslide of my body
And walked into the ocean in my clothes and my reading glasses
With the shit of somebody else tarred on my elbows and lap,
In the stench of their soft blockage, the stink of their panic attack.
Come back! they called me, *Come here!* – as if they were synonyms.
But I stood my ground in the shoreline, in this artist's smock
  of a shirt,
And the waves were the colour of matchlight struck in the uterus
When the Anglo-Saxon explorer discovers the treasure-house is
  his tomb.
There, in the valleys of useless unceasing, in a lost continent,
Atlantis at last unfolded and folded before me.
The sand was slipping in flutes from my foothold. Hollows welled up.
I stripped like a skinny mystic, a born-again vegan,
Who lives in the love of the Holy Ghost with the white lice in
  his armpit,

Who has left the bodies of women for the washed body of Christ,
And finds himself at sea then in the groundswell of his shallows.
All that his baffled eardrum hears is the labour of bodily breathing.
The water lops at his waist. My image was leaking like semen
And the children were chanting a name I was given at birth
In the odours of myrrh and chaplain's tobacco and groomed bed-linen
And the flaps of my mother's ruined vagina.
They were singing like seals, like mermaids, like men and women.
The taste in my mouth was the smell of my eyes in the small hours.
Then I waded in wholly, where the waves caved in on me,
With my genitals in my hands like something the sea had thrown up,
All slick with the oils of God knows what, the fish-scales, the feathers,
My two ridiculous nipples hardened to things
And the hairs on my body standing up straight to be counted.'

'Are you reading still those seventy-seven lost plays of Sophocles?
The sum of such calamity is the arithmetic of hairs.
Was that pantry-maid anorexic, a child assuming flesh,
When Rubens portrayed her as sumptuous, all milk and genitals?
That would be called bereavement by one who was flesh and blood.
And the third wife of Milton, did she truly puncture her eardrums
When the *Fee Fi Fo Fum* of his voice had diminished to tinnitus?
She could not get him out of her head, you see. He had gone to
ground there.
If it were not for you, would I know anything of all these
Table-quiz arcana that have magnified now into mysteries
Like the mineral water I hear at night in your bedroom
Tinkling like filaments still on the other side of the handle?

Pure spirits dissolve like alcohol. They are next to nothing –
No hair in the black star of the sink, no nicotine smell in the
wardrobe,
No zero of lacquer on the bed-board from the read halves of novels.
The hospital chaplain photocopied photocopies of prayers
Yet I would bring you back into this wall-fallen world,
No beeswax Book of Hours but a book of soft matches.
Sophocles could start all over his history of the Bosphorus,
Blindcraft and bloodshed, while that housekeeper of genius,
Turning a deaf ear to the protestations of Paradise,
Would listen to the field-mice frequencies of turf going up in smoke;
And Rubens's waif, climbing her feeding-tube like a rope-ladder,
Should sign in deaf and dumb for the bowl of painted apricots.
Climb into the car again where the rain's diagonal javelins
Travel so hard my lips can't hear what my lungs are breathing.
Your hair smells of the months that have ended in ember

As I pick the gravel path from the jelly of your eyebrow
And promise you help with your Greek, help with your English, help.
You are making the animal sounds somebody taught you,
The iambic mammal whimperings of a trapped, baffled calf,
Which maddens the mothers on the other side of the hedgerow
Till they charge the green undergrowth and go straight into it –
The whiplash, slashing, heart-destroying arsenal –
Though the drudgery of their udders drags like a skull in bandages.'

'Eichmann on retreat in the Catholic monastery
Was right when he talked of a Jewish conspiracy.
That monument on the Île de France,
The ashes in Salonica, the flame in Florence –
The whole of Europe is a pauper's grave,
A Jewish plot from Le Havre to the Sea of Azov.
Thank God that my over-extended family
Hosted two refugees on their way to Galilee
When they were not the people with whom one hobnobbed;
And that the Vice-Commodore of the yacht club
Regretted the blackballing of an Anglo-Saxon sort
Who would tan like a bedouin on any golf course.
It means I can hold my head up a little
When I visit the camp whose impossible middle
Begins with an A and ends with a Zed
On day three of my crowded Kraków schedule,
Or when I arrange the return visit somehow
Of the InterSwap steering committee, at Dachau.
If I bring the kids, we might even travel
To the castle where they shot the musical
Chitty Chitty Bang Bang, and my daughter
Literally shitted herself at the rat-catcher's
Slow walk with the bullwhip and bird cage
Down the cobbled streets where the children waited.
I can't remember the rest of the plot.
Great gas, though. I must say I applaud
Any Jew thick-skinned enough to sink money
In a movie made after all in Germany.
It shows them for the entrepreneurs that they are.
Business as usual. There's no smoke without fire –
Einstein, Groucho Marx. They're everywhere.
No wonder the monks said we haven't a prayer.'

SONG FOR THE STUDENT NURSES

When you skipped among shallow graves
In your gypsy skirts and sneakers
It was not because you were saviours
But because of exams before Easter.

I thought of the child in *Frankenstein*
In her pretty pastel smock
Who was not, and could not have been, shocked
While the monster held her like china

And the villagers made their escape
In a Transylvanian panic;
But the drooling toddler draped
Flowers on his manacled ankles.

You also brought green garlands,
Lavender too for the long nights;
Rounders after heavy rainfall,
The home-base marked by your bright cardigans.

So may you continue
Kissing our toads back into princes;
No matter how slim the chances
May your mezzo laughter win through

To the whole of us, to the wholeness in us,
We who store skeletons
In our abdomens, the outlines of infants,
Abortions we breastfeed.

ST HELEN'S FLOOR

That old man's empire has eroded now
To seminars with a toddler from down the corridor
On a strategy straight from *De Bello Gallico*
As his toothpick massacres the sugar substitutes.

In order to encompass all of him like a continent
His son must invade Russia at four miles an hour.
Snow will settle on him its sad alcohol. Soon
His feet will be bandaged in his dad's death notices.

REQUIEM FOR A ROOMMATE

What does the priest do after the funeral Mass?
The rest of us drive in the hills that we call mountains
Or walk the pier where the boys in their knickerbockers
Posed for the Lawrence collection in the Museum –
Silverfish dangle from their fishing rods, the nineteenth century
Lights on their hands and their hair but their eyes are in darkness –
And the crinoline women awaiting the change of life
Tuck three serviettes in the hairy blood of their bottom.

We stand in the hall of our home on the swell of the carpet
As home-sick as our great-grandparents on any breakwater.
The children must put themselves to bed from now on.
Their clothes lie inside-out where they used to kneel
For their rhyming prayers, while the couple who made them up
Warm their hands on the hair-dryer before we can bear to touch –
My grand-uncle's face in your great-grandmother's fingers –
And offer up our genitals as if they were oxygen masks.

But the priest in his presbytery who prayed to the back of his hands
And lifted up the Gospel to be greeted in song,
Must now fill in five minutes between two sub-committees.
Darkness blackens the window like any old day in his diary.
He sits in the pub-smoke smell of his underwear, lasting.
There will be no child to suck the taste from his cigarette-finger
Or watch the worms his hands flashburn while he hooks them
For the sight of one salmon bursting free from the fishkill.

HANDICAP

You are always the first for Holy Communion
Though you take it out of your mouth then to inspect it
Like a postage stamp from some old, abolished country –
Iraq, say, when it was British Petroleum.
We cannot drink from your chalice and that is because
You leave bubbles in it, bobbing nasal secretions.

How did you make it through the curfew and the checkpoints,
The night-vision of border guards, the doctors
Asleep in their stethoscopes under the alphabet chart?
That lorry's undercarriage smelled of oranges
Or the woman who hid you in her field of vision
Handed a sheepdog's afterbirth to the priests on horseback.

Now you are the last Eskimo to speak Aleut,
The last Ethiopian to make love in Italian,
The last altarboy to pray in Latin for his own angina.
Open your lips and I shall proclaim the praise
Of your bad buck teeth like a desecrated graveyard
Where the Hebrew runs backward, the letters of ambulance.

Like the runner from Marathon you are dying to tell us
A battle has been won: it is all Greek from here on,
Beauty of form contents us. I don't move a muscle.
Here in the driver's seat I'm home again, home again,
While he circles the car in his crazy electric chair,
Calling: Aidan, Aidan, if that is you, will you tell me?

AEGIS

The gulls had eaten in no time at all
The soft parts of the face with Down's syndrome

And picked too at the stitches of lambswool
On the jersey rescuers judged must be a sheep.

I remember my Aran sweater filling like armour
When I turned turtle in a sea-scouts' test of endurance

And that first sodden body I helped to manhandle
Into the mortuary, like a blanket-chest on a landing.

I might have been swept out to sea myself since then
To the far side of creation and been washed up

In Japan, even, where they call the Mongoloids English
Who are only dyed in the wool of Leviticus.

Yet whether the patterns that criss-cross my chest
Say lamb of god, black sheep or stench of scapegoat,

Wolf in a kid's clothes, mutton dressed as ram,
They are the threads which would bring it all home again

To hands that are knitting still by a shoreline of firelight
And smaller hands hanking the ball till it's shipshape

On a boy's two wrists raised high like a swimmer
Surrendering, wading in up to the navel in pain.

Be it Isaac the palmist or your man Polyphemus,
Combing and combing in their stranded states,

Who frisks his bumpy tunic that was the gulls' tablecloth,
His face and fingerprints would still pull the wool over

The world's eyes. Most welcome? Most wanted?
Imagine their likeness is like nothing on earth,

Oceans away from our wool-gathering margins,
The straits in which we find ourselves. Imagine

That the breakwaters fleece them as they run aground,
That we flock to see it happen with our sheep's eyes.

THE BURNT OFFERING

The sun sinks in the West like a monk in saffron
Who has sat all day in the stone garden at the fossils of chimneys
Until feeling has gone from his legs and his loins and his solar plexus.
Now the mosquito drills for her legal millilitre on his phalanges;
And the common temple-spider crosses his eyelash like a rope-bridge,
Portering ice-picks and pain-killer for the Europeans
Who have moved mountains to come to this, their last ashram
  by gaslight.

GENESIS

Abraham saw them coming. He stood up and met them halfway,
The three men of Mamre. He had been studying acorns
Lying around the guy-strings and the sheep-droppings,
And there they were, the holy trio, full-grown in front of him,
An old man cross-legged at the flap of his sheepskin tent.
All it lacks is the moment of myrrh and frankincense,
This epiphany of the three faiths that flow from one walkabout,
The natal moment of Israel and of the Lamb and of Islam.
So Abraham brings water and he washes their bare feet for them.

Their heads are haloed by horseflies that have zeroed in.
The sun behind their hoods shadows them like a bodyguard
And the oak trees stand their ground in perfect obedience
As the sand hardens to glass and the glass melts into moisture.
His tongue has swollen with thirst like a pebble for public speaking.
What they tell him is a heat-haze, it is water vapour condensing.
Abraham's body deepens like a well as he drinks
Adventures of strangeness and of consolation,
A cataract in the stalactites of his skeleton.

He washes their feet as if he were watering roots,
The tattoo picked out neatly like a Singer sewing machine might
And the flagellated soles of the alien colonial
And the third man's fallen arches, his crippled heel of Achilles
With a weal from a knotted bootlace on the instep like a birthmark
Targeting the carpentry of the torturer. He is that pedestrian,
The shoeshine of the foot-loose, of the footsore trinity
Who have walked so far to meet him in his intercessions
They have feet of clay as wizened as the two soles of a foetus.

PATERNOSTER

Our fathers are far beyond us. We cannot divine them.
Their names are taken in vain as a middle initial
When we autograph our forgeries on a child's homework
Or open a passport's proof at the unspeaking night-desk.
Watch them retreating now into their vast futures.
How can we turn those Russias, those Americas,
Estates that curve with the world like roots at a riverbank,
Into Monaco, say, and her pre-set soda sprinklers?
No kingdoms then. No Kaisers, Tsars or Caesars,
Yet a stone's throw, a spit from where we're standing,
God in a nappy holds his privy council,
The unearthly, earthen father.

Give us this day
The sight of them at their breakfast television
To break our hearts like a breadloaf and feed our babies
Who cannot ever imagine how we invented them
In the wedding dress of our mystical skin and hair.
My marriage and my children forgive our fathers
Everything I have done thus far. Let us believe then –
In the face of the facts of life and the death of fiction –
In our great-granddaughters' deliverance, in our great-granddaughters,
And in the temptation that we are leading them there.
The lingerie, the loincloths, our enormous wardrobe:
It has all summoned the truthful body to evidence.
Now we begin it as well, our descent into ancestry.

Somewhere beyond the last of our prepositions
There may be a still from a film in which we are shown
With our curious hairstyles circled in haloes like hit-lists
As a strange class of forebears smiles at the twenty-first century:

There's a dimple's origin, a lobe's long genealogy.
They will stare till Kingdom come at our powerlessness and
 our glory.
They will look death in the face, us, neither son nor sir,
Their fathers so far within them they cannot be human.

WHEN

When we have killed the last priest,
The last skinflint supremo of hard-core
And the snowman selling icicles in the schoolyard,
There will be peace, I suppose, or at least an armistice.
Aspirin will clear in the fluoridated water
And the halogen lights come on over the swimming pool
If a bird breaks the beam.

I'm not forgetting foreign arms manufacturers,
Abortionists, anti-abortionists, or the last major
Nazi war-criminal painting nativities in Montevideo.
In the silence of simultaneous translation
They must pay for their silver bullet, their sharpened stake,
The mirrors which return our own reflection: us,
The ordinary gardeners.

Afterwards, as we clean our nails with the sausage sticks,
The windows will repeat the overhead lighting –
Sodium on the thighs and breasts in the freezer – and show us
The glazed sight of ourselves on a hidden camera.
You doing nothing in particular. Me the same.
Our watermarks sitting down among the azaleas
As simply as two refugees.

Now is the time for your own shadows to speak
In their altered voices. How the set flickers like fire!
Run from the courthouse with a coat over your head.
It is too late in the darkness to identify
Cain from his dental records among the button mushrooms
Or Abel's thumbprints on the kitchen gloves
He rinsed under threadworms of tapwater.

PHOTO-OPPORTUNITY

James and John, the place-men par excellence,
Are heart-set on being bumped up to the high table.
Who will preside at his right hand and who at his left
While the Politburo claps until their palms are aching?

Up there three bodies bend in the foetal position.
On the left the rape-and-murder man is shitting bricks;
Right of him sobs the paedophile who's found Jesus.
And torn between shit and piss like a burst perineum

The Son of Man is utterly alone, a mother's son
Who stood once in the A-frame of her legs like a doorpost
And saw beyond Galilee on either side of him
The presscorps aiming and shooting and reloading.

CHAPTER HEADINGS FOR A BIOGRAPHY

The first
Being the autograph of his life to a lethal adolescence
In the which he is always and everywhere mocked and maltreated
By parents and by godparents and by God the Ghost.

The second
In which the foregone gospel truth is rendered in sing-song
And the sing-song scissored from newsprint like an obituary,
His photostats sobbing toward a portfolio.

The third
Wherein our heterodox hero abandons all doxa for Heterosoc
And all Platonic relationships for the working parties of Aristotle,
First with Felicity, then with Dolores.

The fourth:
An entrance antiphon for the hallway's good theology
And the romanesque acoustic of unfurnished rooms
Where smalltalk sweetens, sometimes, to a sung liturgy.

The fifth –
On a weekend pass a triumph of modern medication
Lifts up his living image to the sage and aged orang-utans
While his wife fumbles in her handbag for the jammed Kodak.

The sixth
In which he kisses the palms of his father's hands and blesses
The tiny atrocities of the house-dust mite
And the mice among the breadcrumbs at the Last Supper.

The seventh
Heaven of animal and vegetable and mineral
That rests on us like a skullcap, phylacteries, a prayer shawl,
The world's weight on our shoulders.

TOTAL IMMERSION

In my second life
I want to be decanted as two atoms
Of hydrogen and one of air you can sing to.

My eager, evergreen rivers would
Fatten the lapping capitals,
The kids wade into me beyond their umbilicus.

Such cloudshapes I would stage on sabbaths,
Army convoys would stop in their trucks,
The nuncio cable Rome,

And amateur painters on *Autobahnen*,
Agog at the Tabor truth of my colours,
Forget the numbers for field-grey and azure:

I would be black and blue for them,
Yet the winter sun would pierce me through,
A laser of light, a picture of innocence.

On the benevolent I would fall as snow,
On the evil, even on Mozart's murderer,
I would settle as drizzle.

Men in the shabby bedlam of stetls,
Their foreheads grimy as anthracite miners,
Would angle their cheeks like schoolchildren

For many swift kisses. Then
In my passing, my passion, my pietà,
The world's slate would be wiped like a window.

Meantime I am happy to be
A puddle at the zebra,
Too muddy to look up anyone's underwear,

Or even a Tupperware what-you-may-call-it
Of drinking water left at a heater
To dampen down the atmosphere

And shiver at the sudden sound-waves
Of a girl in a bed-sit dropping, thud,
First one espadrille, thud, then the other.

NIGHT LIGHTS FROM LORCA

I SPINSTER AT PRAYER

The incense has been impregnating
Your hair and handbag. Wake from your fortywinks.

Duck at the bearded saint. Duck at the bald one.
Smoke flocks like pigeons where the bread was broken.

Foderunt manus meas et pedes meos.
The pins and needles; the tongue's long neuralgia.

One bead. Another. Your rosary weeps
Tears in your lap like a punnet of raisins.

You have lost count of the dates, of the decades.
Ages of Latin are all so much Greek to you

And your head droops in a flimsy mantilla
As fine as any chemise in a trousseau;

But you ooze on an ancient flannel scrap
The smell of a scrubbed anatomy room:

Even the sacristan scented it
As he corkscrewed wax from candlestick sockets.

Christ in a foodstall bawled when he swallowed
Olive oil for the pus in a nipple.

II SOFT DAY

The women groom begonias at the window-sill.
The alley's wringing. They inhale through their lipstick

The lane's damp places, mould, unlaundered muslin,
The mint from a pantry rubbed in their armpits' stubble.

Evaporation like incense! Thurible of the globe!
Whose mound-of-the-pubis presses the wet wrought-iron

Guard-rail of the balcony? She lets the militia
The small moons of her nails, a silkworm tourniquet cuff,

And the perpendicular coldsore of sweat
That slides to her stomach like the chain of a medal.

But the crewcut, quickstep conscripts prance past her.
Their trenchcoats steam like quicklime at a mass burial.

III DEADWOOD

Woodsman,
Make light of my shadow.
Spare me this nightmare,
The sight of no fruit at all.

Morning and evening
The sunlight sees through me
But the tiny decimals
Of the stars are more decent.

Armies of insects
Have camped in my branches,
And the chant of the tom-tit
Is an ant's pitter-patter.

Woodsman, I ask
For the mercy of metal:
Reprieve of the hatchet,
Relief of the saw.

IV SICKBED

If I die of my body – always depending
Like the cardboard dormers of the house-martins –
Jemmy the window, elbow the eaten putty.
Make a fist of your two hands for a leg-up.

A toddler's peeling some class of apricot
Like a spiral staircase. He is south-south-east of me.
He spits a shaggy pit-stone from his wet goatee
In the steamburned palm of his ironing sister;

And a farmhand savages leaky beetstalks –
Let a fluke slipstream airmail me
The scent of his skin like an old watchstrap
With two burst holes for his granddaughter's wrist.

Swifts have no sandals. The shod orderlies
Are airing my mattress. Shoulder these shutters
From their jammed latches, their whitewash jackets
Like slapstick shell on a helmeted fledgling.

FACE TO FACE

Even the handkerchief you leave your mark on –
Sputum from the pleurisy you're almost proud of,
Semen from a cock-up in the bed-and-breakfast
And the odd tears too with the awful bottle-end sea-smell –
Has somebody else's initials on it. They were there already
Before you learned your letters, those written-off outpourings.
They had been in the family for ages, in the blanket-chests
With the parachute bed-sheets that the prostitutes laundered
Along with this handkerchief and its washed-out embroidery –
Spring flowers or a harvest bonnet – that your father could offer
Like a purificator to a patient in tears.
And how will we ever know which came first in the face-to-face,
Veronica's napkin soaking up the Holy of Holies
Or the veil of the Temple torn into strips for bandages?

THE HEAD APPEARS

It seems he has been resting there for a whole lifetime,
Surrounded by hands with the give-away ghosts of wedding rings
And a bled torpedo of oxygen.

It is over for her. The birth of the brain
Is the huge nativity. The birth of the body is no great matter.
A child in a swimming pool

Shoulders out of the water because it has started to rain.
She thinks of the painting lessons she likes on the radio,
Of cigarettes, stitches.

He is head over heels in love with what he can sense,
Her slippery, red-blooded, man-handled understudy
In his arseways universe –

The collar of her muscles throttling his jugular
And the pubic stubble with the toilet odour of estuaries
Where kids bury their dads in sand –

But he knows zero. He has never gazed on her navel,
Or caught her breasts' expression. That faraway face might be
An animal's or an astronaut's.

So they lie there for an eternity under the overhead glare.
The woman has always insisted on this room, this roll-call.
Daniel. Dan. Aidan.

The wadded, quadriplegic weight of him in her.
All he is sure of are the bloodshot maps on his eyelids,
Their salt-water tributaries

And the tortuous, two-headed creatures with pleurisy
Whose New World woodcuts sold the sixteenth century.
Monks too had heard shrieking

And held up the host as they rowed past the whirlpool
To a girl with gouged lips from whose skinned behind emerged
The badgerstripe scalp

Of someone who would go back if he could to the very beginning
To find out how it all ended, to shoulder those split, infinite
Seconds and then head off home.

WORKING THROUGH THE NIGHT

for G

We've synchronised our anticlockwise watches,
You in Melbourne and me in a village in Dublin,
Though the question-mark that hangs over my life
Is not the Plough but a yellow star from heaven.

Now I can imagine you driving to your patients,
To the clean, chainsmoking shirts, the dirty hair
While I sit here chewing the last of the nicotine tabs
In this stargazing, radiant study I call my canvas.

Above the waterline of the washing-machine
The hull of the house curves to the rooms of children.
The two of us steer by such meteors, chartered flights,
The odd illegal firework and the same radio chopper

Telling our galley kitchens what the traffic will come to.
You've bought your own son a telescope too
As large as the one that made a supernova blaze
Out of a halogen light on a lawn up in Stepaside.

While you walk the child till his crying finds its stride
I undress in birdsong and postman's bronchitis.
Moonlight and sunlight sometimes surprise them together,
Our kids' clothes heaped on their carpets like goal-posts.

Which of our wheels within wheels will come full circle?
Like Abraham, the daddy of all long legs,
We've both left country, family, family home,
For the background radiation on the medium wave.

Besides, you're expatriate from the time you shave,
An emigrant at your daughter's menstruation
And an exile when your heart sinks like a root
In the lithosphere that was once a small allotment.

'The green planets is growing inside in our garden,'
My daughter said. Her lips were golden with ice-pop.
Now your kids storm through, wearing their grandparents,
And crying in Australian at the open mouth of Ireland

While my own wrangling language – am, amn't, am –
Walks out on my night-life in the middle of a sentence
And writes things down that I never could imagine,
Yahweh and *Fuck*, that used to be dashes and stars.

INTERCESSIONS

Morning and evening prayer on top of the Bible,
My chock-a-block office at the start of year B –
No wonder we've hardly talked since that Torah Talmud
When my body was liquidated in flesh and blood.

I have not forgotten. I am your remembrance of me.
My true-life fictions are out in Czech and Slovak
But the card on my father's table is a ballpoint fib.
I hold his hand just to tell him the time on his watch;

It's a stranger studies his thumbnails like a bulletin.
Then there's the other. Poems I've written my wife –
Those solemn intimacies occur among advertisements
Like the shadow between a stocking and a stretchmark

Though I read the editorials in our marriage bed.
Our zigzag, dogsbody dialogue is no different, Lord.
Wherever I go, our correspondence ends
In the imagery and unlikelihood of my halfway house –

The children that leave me, the children that remain.
Among women who sweat blood and men who shed it
I have hidden the good news here and there in the small print,
The stop-press headlines in the births and deaths.

CAEDMON

Because I could sing to high heaven,
The abbot made me. Marched to the altar,
Shotgun-style by a scalping party,
My head felt eery, an oval shaved off
As if for delicate neurosurgery.
What were they thinking beyond in the buttery,
My mates in the shepherds' dormitory
As I bent my neck, as I bent my knee?
'Sing me Creation', says the Master of Novices,
The making of matter, a seven-day wonder,
The universe forming from misty gases
Like a Disprin dropped in a glass of water;
'Sing me the Exodus out of Egypt,'
The sulphur springs of the promised land.
And I try, I cry out from my mouthful of cavities
In the midst of the statues that throw their eyes upwards
Blindly towards Paradise. I am gargling bog Latin
Like salt sea-water for runny ulcers.
Still, in a month of Sundays, a full church calendar,
I'll never be home here.
                                        What I want instead
Is the benediction of words like cabbage
Out in the back where the plot is thickening;
And the lipservice I languish for
Is no chanted canticle but an oral tradition,
My wife with the dental anaesthetic
Turning the other cheek as I mount her.
Because this is it: when the accurate image
Cools and clears in the sacred mysteries
Like an egg-white whitening in the pan,
It is her curved spaces in the settle beside me
The sun, the moon and the stars shine out of,
These that I take to my heart and husband
Wholly, wholly, wholly.

WAY OUT

The people of God are at snail's pace on the carriageway.
Men empty soot from their shavers out the driver's window;
The women put on lipstick. Their mouths in the mirrors pout,
Part and make-up like opera singers in a silent movie.

For whom shall the Angel of Death come down today
In this bumper-to-bumper stillness on the Via Sacra?
For the breadline at the bus-stop, the students with buckets,
Or the old lady who looks like good Pope John in a Fiat?

Whose cheeks will darken tonight in the mortuary chapel?
He is listening now to a cricket result from Australia.
Whose net of mandarins will be written down with a number?
Her hands smell of her breakfast and the steering wheel.

Maybe myself, for all the Holy Communion
Of tablets taken clockwise, a diet of small red sandstone,
Will be the one to finish up like a desert father
With my corneas and kidneys in a silver slop-bowl.

Yet spare me, Lord, so long as it takes my book
Of hunger strikes and illuminated manuscripts
To be bigger than Kells, brighter by far than Kundera,
The book of 6, The Fairways, Woodbrook Glen. Then only

Let my acids enrich the eucalyptus – but for now
Take you my own wife's brother (a shit) or one of the consuls
With their Argyll socks full of anti-fungal powder
Or those who believe they've seen God on a mountain,

Never in a valley. Our first-world fortysomethings
Have bodies that wrinkle into better and better maps –
Let their contact lenses guide them towards their graves,
Their wedding rings be shaped into crowns for cavities.

But spare the children, the childlike, spare even the childish,
Who hang from their parents to shit on the traffic island,
And some of the able-bodied, the ones with phantom limbs –
I mean three people – whose deaths repeat in them like sea-food.

LAUDS

You have turned my laments into dancing,
You have stripped off my sackcloth.

Psalm 30

THE NIGHT SHIFTS

At the end of all my days, Compline or close-down,
The nights begin: seven, of course, the same as Genesis
But one of me at two in the morning for the great Amens.
Sunday I wake to the wet between us, a daughter asleep
Where we ruined the sheets on the night of her conception.
The blanket she breathes was knitted by mantelpiece pictures.
Monday you stitch it. Threads that you straighten criss-cross
The powder prints of my footsteps' stepping-stones
To a crib where I hold my nails at a toddler's nostrils.

The air in motion. Tuesday. The night shifts like a wind.
Out at the valeted car, where the ants manhandle breadcrumbs,
A wheelchair shines like a throne in the keyhole cul-de-sac.
And on Wednesday night a doorknob, a drawstring, a strip-bulb –
You gargle in your pelt such strange sinkhole arpeggios
And your mirror-image magnifies more than the sight of you.
Thursday. The wallswitch in our last pebbledash home
Ghosts the palm of my hand like a washed telephone number:
The wick in the votive shrine is the red alert of a pilot.

Friday you saddle my breast-bone like a coronary –
Stretchmarks, snap-lines, body and blood of a stranger
Whose drop-earrings quieten now at the creak of wicker.
I licked your body then like condensation in Sinai
Though the neighbours were leaving their houses when the TV
  told them to,
Barefoot in their dressing-gowns for the meteor that would miss us.
Imagine them stretching the pleats of their eyelids to see it!
Imagine the rabbit slippers, the stocking-masks of vaseline,
The soft black blindfolds against streetlight, the Santa binoculars,
And the man who put the bins out under the supernova.
Here is the whole host of heaven. Here is a six-day wonder.

It all adds up to a Saturday, to the sound of recorders
And the night-nurse drawing her blinds for the day to colour
in water.
Weight in eternity. The days will weaken toward us
With little revelations. While the aged hallucinate
And the candles are lit against the quick smell of their sweetness,
We lie in a way that is not untruthful, in a nonfiction legend,
Where the light will show the curtains up for the lining they lack
And the laundry-basket's deposits amount to Jericho
While the children stand round the bed as if we were sinking.

ADDED ON TO THE ROOM

They had omitted the thirteenth floor in our hotel.
The cleaning woman we met in the service stairwell
Between the twelfth and the fourteenth downward spiral
Was an Armenian. Numbers were lost on her.
She carried keys in her hand like the fisherman mosaic.
When I stopped to inhale you under your coat we could hear,
Flight after flight, the slow clap of her flip-flops
Above and beyond us.

You had gone out into the city without underwear
To pick wildflowers in the fields around St Martin's.
When we came back, an Indian *femme de menage*
Was stacking boots whose writing on the insoles
Dissolved in sweatstains like a footsore marriage
And you had left my shoes among them on the door-saddle.
But we were different. We were finger-painting
At the right room-temperature

Each other's species in the dust of the city
As if it were flour and the floor was a baker's dozen.
The rest is history. When tired Korean maids
Folded our bed-sheets, a red dot in a white field,
I knew about the sun and the sun rising, and said so.
It has taken me thirteen years to salute a skirt
That flags in its brown bloodstain on a wire washing-line
The lace-work of our moccasins.

ADVENT

A single lightbulb will keep a room from freezing
And a hairsbreadth of water from the tap in the kitchen
Is a thread for the whole household to follow safely.
So we are hopeful. We are not full of hope.

The small of your back still looks like seven years ago
But your face was not protected from the light falling
And the total eclipse of the moons of your fingernails
Was the forecast of darkness as our only hard surface.

Yet the sentences you write me end in prepositions,
The behaviour of January, twigs like TV aerials;
I am coming on out from in under myself
To stand in the warm slipstream of your solid ground,

In the apostolic succession of flesh and blood,
Of bodies squeezed from bodies that were squeezed from bodies
Before them in the landlocked scheme of our brokenness.
I would go in and out of you like your children have

But that is for later. That is the fullness of time
And this is slower than hair, the clockwork acoustic of frost
Where I walk in slow motion like those astronauts
To a height I could hardly imagine, the dispensation of tablets.

They had run about in the crater and not looked back,
Agog at the thought of themselves; then there was silence.
Millions below held their breath at the sound of them breathing,
The overheard air, a moistening, nostrils and labia,

For they were crying, the moonmen. They had seen the world,
The blue beyond them. This was their freezing darkness.
And I have looked back too, the lunatic of tick-tocks,
To the basin where we once washed babies and cabbageheads

And to the coolie shade that lit up as we lay down
Out of the blue one night among our dead and our dying
For the pillar of salt and the tower of strength to share there
Each other's thirst, each other's drinking water.

OUT OF THE ARK

Night-time. Light winds. Our nautical attic tacks
In the creaking of planks as if we were bunking down
On a dry spinnaker under a gurgling fo'csle,
As if the great Gulf Stream had carried us out to sea.

Your head on a bolster beside me makes two of us.
Two children are sleeping on beachtowels two doors down.
Out the back a couple of blackbirds ignore two city foxes;
And it is still too early to say if this is all too late

For the second commandment of *love thy neighbour*
And the second law of the science of thermodynamics.
Those stone eggs lugged from the Galapagos Islands
Were the bare bones of our story – fins into feathers,

The fossil record, solitude of sperm-banks –
Yet we set out as Darwin and come home as Noah,
Boat-people now with no Admiralty charts
But a pontoon bridge of cattle-ships and coffin-ships

To disembark us here. Horseshoe shape of a harbour!
Small telescopes, the cardboard tubes of toilet rolls,
Circle our mirror-image, the pair of us in it together,
Doubling the dog-dirt on the hall, stairs, and landing

In this animal house weighed down to the waterline,
This dumb, stumped, unmanoeuvrable tub,
The high point of its ebbing when it ran aground,
Anchored on dirty Ararat like a nipple-ring.

THEE

Weddings first and then christenings and then funerals.
It's as straightforward as subject, verb, object,
This move from the altar to the font to the mortuary chapel.
How it leaves us speechless, how it takes our breath away!
Yet the day I helped to carry my brother's coffin
There was the sound of confetti under my desert boots,
And after the worst two years since our records began,
The cot has come out of our attic like a Jew after a pogrom.
Amid all the bloodshed, we are one flesh assuming it,
At a standstill certainly, uncertainly, but still standing.

At the time of writing, the garden is dead and buried.
But come whenever, Passover say, or at Pentecost,
The kids will be playing Mass with their chocolate buttons,
Inventing miracle stories out of the telephone book
Where the ivy has gone and greened the cable for Cable TV
And the blackbird returns to her nest with a drinking straw from
  a Coke;
And I will be there, observing their serving, giving thanks
For our dying days in the land of the living; thanksgiving
For this indefinite time, this world, this definite article
Pronounced like the ancient form of a pronoun that stands for you.

LAWRENCE O'TOOLE

Priest and prelate, patron saint of the city of Dublin

When I chose your name for mine
From a perfumed bishop at age twelve,
It was for saints who head-and-shouldered
The narrow church of my puberty.

It was for Lawrence of Arabia,
His stare searching me out
In the deep parterre, his hands
Beckoning through the mosquitoes

To a water-hole on the far
Side of the intermission;
And the first Saint Laurence
Whose sangfroid at boiling point

(Turfed onto a gridiron,
Roasting his captors with
'I am done enough on that front,'
The ironist at his rarest)

Was how I would show them all
When grown-up overseas,
My whole family listening in tears
To an update on Father Aidan

At the hands of the Red Chinese,
Shanghai'd in a dungeon.
I am older and wizened, my true patron.
Beyond wanderlust or witness

Your wry, monotonous taste
For the Word in the word-perfect
Ordnance of memoranda
Suits me down to the ground –

'Where were those gutters bought
For the sacristy in Poitiers?
And what of this cut-price calfskin
That has cornered the market in parchment?' –

Like your choice of a job of work,
Raising up Nazareth
In the bustle and dust-clouds
Of a junction of hovels.

For the truth is El Auruns
Counted the stars like sheep,
Yet when sleep came it was English
Meadowsweet he inhaled;

And the fat part of a leg of lamb
That spattered my wrist on Tuesday
Brought it home to me
Men are not witty on a toasting fork.

So, in your low-key clockwork way,
Preferring the punctilio
Of a well-kept parish register,
You tell me straight out. Moonlight,

You say, will make a hencoop even
Gleam like any millennium helmet,
Sunlight stencil a cart-shaft
Arrow-sharp at matins,

Aiming at Heaven. And this, you tell me,
Is weirder, more newfangled
Than camels in the dry stretches,
A saint's holocaust

Or the glass that filled to half-way
Only, obediently on the second
Sunday of Advent
With the colourless tears of Mary Magdalen.

ORIENTATIONS

We make love between the tea-chests on a carpet
That covers the known world and the holes in the rubberback.
Now we have gone and begun it, the journey into the stairwell
Through the keyhole cul-de-sac and the hammer-headed one

Via the weddings and the christenings and the funerals
Of the whole archdiocese. You can see the lights of Vegas
And the great wall of China from the moon's point of view
But a Persian power-cut scaled us down to the one bay window

And a door-chain no stronger than your glasses' string. Look you:
Our sex and violence have been like nothing on earth
And the spectacles we've folded at the four fringed corners
Are the bottle-ends they plaster in the balconies of palaces.

THE DREAM-HOUSE

I can come no closer to your dream-house than this:
The attic has thawed from an igloo to a hay-loft
As the spider regroups its life on the sobbing porthole.
Suppose he is female. Suppose she is there to stay.

It can take you forty years to walk round a garden,
To plant the stubs of your cigarette ration like bulbs.
Now their smoke clears to an armistice of crocuses.
Fat from a slaughtered animal hangs on a line

Between your pilgrim collar and a child's gingham smock,
Its pocket darned from when she walked to school
With sheep's-wool on barbed wire for the nature table.
Listen.The humming. Down the side of the dream-house,

In the arrow-slit passageway between the walls,
A boy strikes shields out of bin-lids in his dream-smithy
While the girls stagger like land-mine amputees
In their orthopaedic ice-skates on the dream-potholes;

And the ghost-writer dreams he is assuming flesh
Where the dove came down at last in the form of a pigeon
Via the skyscraper sea-cliffs of the last Ice Age,
Cathedrals heaped like kelp, the spinnakers of markets,

And the Hapsburg aquatints of a flooded Venice,
To wade in our apple-blossom as if she was landed,
As if there was no such thing as the day before yesterday.
The children clap to scare her. She goes on gorging.

GLINTS

I am seeing the world now through my stained glasses,
Milk and mucus of children on the scratched lenses,
Their greasy scalps streaking the photochrome finish
And my own sweat grouting the sockets with sediment.
Sight for sore eyes! Behold the beholden, me,
Whose tortoise-shells slid down into the underworld
Like the tortoises I buried among deep hydrangeas
And rose again in the blindfolds of breath misting,
The tiny violet venting of this stunned baby.
Her thumb fumbles my eyeball. The room doubles.
A warm saliva washes away my shortsightedness
In the drool and goo of our first thirsty Pentecost.

I am seeing what I can do. I am looking into it
Down the nightmare of groundfog and no visibility
That has brought us weak and wide-eyed into blinding sunlight
And the sight of your fingerprints on the passenger side
Clustered on the windshield to withstand loose chippings
Like the tracks of small animals at a waterhole:
Obstacles returning to the shapes of sheep out there,
Asleep on the tarmacadam as if it were Bethlehem.

RECOVERY

Months among medicines and the messages on bottles
In a bed that lifted and lowered its becalmed canvas,
My head had been walking at low tide round this Ireland,
Stepping into the clay feet of my great grandchildren.

When I pushed my Fiat down the slip of the avenue,
The wipers swathed through the pollen all on their own,
Finding their stroke for the first time and gliding me in,
My head above water, to the oars that shore my attic.

MARTHA AND MARY

I MARY

The only prayer you have is Martha's Magnificat,
Kitchen-sink comedy. You must stand over it
Like a circus diver a hundred feet overhead
Staring down at a watertank as tiny as an inkwell.

Jericho, Troy, the cities of Los Angeles:
The varsity sorts with their tags and toothbrushes
Will tell you all their digs have ended in bedsits,
In taprooms, in the pot-walloping, panhandle world.

Sooner or later you must take the plunge too.
Between the humming freezer and the smoke-signals from kettles
Water wells up. Now your red-handed wrists
In the basin are as beautiful as the Venus de Milo.

II MARTHA

You cannot wash your hands of the water
You wash your hands in. It has come a long way
From the villages at the bottom of the reservoir
To the failed extractor fan of your feature kitchen

Where today – between you, me, and the four walls –
The tiles have misted with the steam of a human encampment.
It's as if you were walking through a cloud on a mountain.
The deep condenses round you in a sac of grey water.

The room is running. Your black-and-blue make-up moistens
And your children write their names on the ghosted windows.
Their signatures weep for the dry eyes in the house,
For what we are part of and parted from, the wet week

That has passed with honour through twenty-five kidneys,
Tumblers with teeth, the bubble tears of lunatics,
Semen, Euphrates, gulags, lagged immersions,
To be the element in which we sink and swim.

PSALMS FOR A MAMMAL

I CHAMBERS

There it lay between vagabond and vagrant.
I declined it through all its cases, the same as *regina*,
A Latin lover locked up in a Vatican state.

It was the mantra of my mid-adolescence.
Imago vaginarum prohibet somnum,
I wrote in my diary. *Domine, excrucior.*

A quarter century later, I turn to *angina*,
A stepping-stone from anger into anguish,
And nominate it vocative of a lifetime.

Tres in diem is what the bottle says,
Nocte on the blister-foil. It is plain language.
Yet whether they speak about marriages

Or love-making, what can such chambermaids
Tell of our ocean from their beachcombing,
Our spherical music from a change of sheets?

Angina, vagina. I write a dogged angel:
'My vague and ongoing heart, the blood you sweat –
Nothing we have done is in the dictionary.'

It is not only age that has made your breasts
Soften towards me. My stubble, much cradle-cap
And the gauntlets of two general practitioners
Have all pavilioned on the high Alban hills –

Remember those Middle English similes
Of snow and milk and semi-precious minerals,
And the goose-bumps on your real areola
Where one hair corkscrewed at my cold sore?

But the soft flesh, the sag in the dear mattress,
Are what bed and embody us. Remember
That doorstep hollowed like an old church font
Where the undergraduates still plunge themselves,

Static of skin, in the sinking of thresholds?
Their foreign tongues are the tongues of angels
Straight out of textbooks from the time we conned them.
They lap it up too, the bountiful Latin.

Bless them and sit astride my pass in History.
The hardness has gone out of me. Remember?
Below the V-neck honey of your suntan, milk-white
Skin that is medieval is grappled for lumps.

III HAIRSBREADTH

Every hair on your head highlights
The dumb blonde with the History double First

Whose long-ago Lady Godiva mane
Like the amber wigwam of an anglepoise lamp

Paraded me through a library at lights-out,
Combing the blur for her centre-parting.

Your axillary hairs tell another story:
You grow them for me from December to March,

The herbal, hibernatory
Life of a lacquered tuft before shortsleeves;

And there's red below that I call Titian
Like light on a twig at the door-frame of the world

In the woodwind of a dwindling night
When you can tell a black thread from a white.

But what am I to do with the grey
Capillaries I picked when I might have been dreaming –

Enough for the tip of a fine paint-brush
To shed light on a pupil observing a hair's breadth –

Or my hands in your numb, unconscious scalp,
As if I were cutting hair from the dead?

IV LONG AFTER CATULLUS

My sweetheart, let us love our life together
Whatever the poormouths say or the cornerboys –
Their smutty chat is nothing to set store by.
Never forget the passage of the seasons,
The way they teach us to etcetera;
Never forget we're fucked for ever after.
So give me your lips, your mouth, your saffron tongue too,
Your small teeth smelling of a mandarin orange,
And kiss me countlessly, kiss me all over,
Your spittle on my chest, my cheeks, my stomach,
Till even the Peeping Toms are lost for language,
Their innuendo at a no-can-do –
Nothing they say translates our speechlessness.

Mensa

The Mass in English and our flesh in Latin –
It takes a lifetime to be sinful and luminous.
We've been declining for years an immense word
That alters and turns the tables on us. You hardly
See it at times for the food that isn't finished,
A service laid in matchsticks and menorahs,
In what might be a vocative – O table of ours! –
Or the muddy ablative life of kids enlarging.

Amo

At the same time we are conjugating, love,
The first verb we have learned from start to finish
In the present, in the imperfect, in the unconditional.
Such language there has been out of the two of us!
It all stems from the mystical phoneme Om,
From page one of a primer with block capital
Autographs hacked out like hearts in wood there,
And a dust-jacket the school-lunch smells amassed.

The fishermen would not lie down with their wives
On the night before they sailed to the herring fields,
For their whole lives would pass in front of them then
Like the ebb unveiling an estuary at low tide
If they brought the salt of the earth to the salt of the sea.

In the small hours when the engine's vibrations
Bring them their bodies heard through a heaped-up pillow,
The painstaking, the prehistoric stroke of it,
The sea remains the sea. The land leans into it.
What happens between them is a line drawn in the sand.

Yet the metrical nets gasp as they enter the water
Like a swimmer crying quietly as he cradles himself
Or a candidate for baptism in her parachute gown.
Something is surfacing. Something is deepening.
There is no telling at all where likeness will lead us two.

That time we made love after we swam in the sea
Was the other way round. Our children were scaling
Fish-nets rigged as a combat-course in the playground;
But the glass-bottomed boats had cut all their motors
And floated like native canoes towards the creaking of sheets.

One tenth of one percent of what we hear
In the saliva and spit of breakfast radio

Is the universe as the Holy Ghost exhaled it.
It's not so much a high helium note,

More like your mother's gasping with bronchitis,
The static of her room in two-star darkness

Or the walkie-talkie crackle from the kitchen
Of my bachelor bacon sliding in a skillet.

Listen to the dancer in the wings inhale
Pure oxygen plus a ciggie. That's it exactly –

She's psyched up for the fanfare, the big brass,
For the leap into the arms that will be there

To lower her into the world and stand her ground –
Kisses, the breathlessness of childbirth,

Pleurisy and the plumage of her carbons –
In the good woodwind, in the hushed house.

WEARINGS

My mother's wedding dress, its moment of almond,
Whitened the walk-in attic like a confetti of petals
Showered through loose roof-slates and the slow ruin of rafters.

It was ripped apart and cut down to size for my sister
Who wore it to her first Holy Communion, and afterwards
Wrapped it away in a wardrobe, enveloped in crêpe.

Later it would shrink to the scale of a christening shawl,
Rent and rented again like the veil of the Temple
To swaddle the puking, sacrosanct manchild;

And the last light that it shed was as a mantilla
Vamoosed out of a church after Benediction
To dress burns on a card-table at an executor's sale;

Like the fishing-net the Virginia creeper crept through
In the bistro that was a fort at the top of the mountain
Where, if you lifted your head and looked out the arrow-slit,

You could see the valley whitening with April,
Hedgerows, orchards, lanes, bits of old bushes,
As if the bridegroom were about to arrive from nowhere.

Our costume changes, our drab vested interests –
How can we match the watercolours of spring
Like the whitebread lying around for the lack of baskets?

Into that healed pavilion of our blossoming,
The rags-to-riches story of shreds laid side by side,
The dress is sewn. It is seamless. It is something else.